sports coach
UK
The National Coaching Foundation

what is sports coaching?

CORNWALL COLLEGE
LEARNING CENTRE

D0543517

ISBN 1 902523 51 2

Based on material from *The Coach in Action* (second edition)
© The National Coaching Foundation, 1996 (ISBN 0 947850 95 3)

Author: Andy Miles
Editor: Nicola Craine
Sub-editor: Warwick Andrews
Designer: Leanne Taylor

Cover photo courtesy of actionplus sports images
All other photographs courtesy of **sports coach UK** and actionplus sports images

Published on behalf of
sports coach UK by

sports coach UK
114 Cardigan Road
Headingley
Leeds LS6 3BJ
Tel: 0113-274 4802 Fax: 0113-275 5019
E-mail: coaching@sportscoachuk.org
Website: www.sportscoachuk.org

Patron: HRH The Princess Royal

Coachwise Solutions
Coachwise Ltd
Chelsea Close
Off Amberley Road
Armley
Leeds LS12 4HP
Tel: 0113-231 1310 Fax: 0113-231 9606
E-mail: enquiries@coachwisesolutions.co.uk
Website: www.coachwisesolutions.co.uk

Contents

contents

sports coach UK

Introduction

The role of sport in society is evolving from its traditional educational and health-related roots into a large money-making industry and, increasingly, a political tool used in anti-crime and anti-drug initiatives. With this expansion comes the increased need for qualified people who can make sport a safe, enjoyable and rewarding experience.

Coaches play a crucial role within sport and can have a significant influence on the participants they coach. Coaching is about developing and improving people and their behaviour within a sporting context. It's also about creating an appropriate environment in which sport can take place.

The process by which coaches achieve this is referred to as the *coaching process* and consists of three main principles (see Figure 1):

- Plan
- Do
- Review.

Figure 1: The coaching process

This resource provides an invaluable introduction to coaching for new and potential coaches, or anyone who simply wants to find out more about what coaching involves. Subjects covered include:

- the roles and responsibilities of the coach

- the coaching process

- motives for coaching

- coaching styles

- coaching skills

- coaching knowledge.

- Throughout this resource, the pronouns he, she, him, her and so on are interchangeable and are intended to be inclusive of both males and females. It is important in sport, as elsewhere, that both genders have equal status and opportunities.

- Although the emphasis of this resource is on coaching, it is aimed at all those who lead or deliver sports programmes (eg coaches, leaders, teachers, instructors, development officers, officials, administrators, volunteers, parents/carers) and those with responsibility for the organisation of sport (eg national governing bodies, local authorities, centre managers, sports clubs).

sports coach UK

Role of the coach

In general terms, a coach is someone whose actions take other people forwards in some aspect of their lives. In a sporting context, a coach is someone who uses sport as a vehicle for the development of individuals, both as performers and as people.

As a coach you can influence the development of your participants in several ways:

- **Technically** by developing good technique and learning new skills.

- **Physically** by improving physical condition and developing good all-round health.

- **Socially** by learning to cooperate and compete with others.

- **Psychologically** by learning to control emotions and develop self-esteem.

- **Personally** by promoting their own welfare, learning life skills and how to manage personal affairs (eg education, careers, socialising), developing sound values and attitudes (eg self-discipline, good manners and politeness).

You are likely to fulfil a variety of roles depending on the participants you work with. These may include:

- **trainer**
- **instructor**   } (helping participants to develop new skills)
- **teacher**

- **scientist** (using the latest knowledge to inform practice)

- **motivator** (encouraging participants to do their best)

- **manager** (managing the development of participants and others).

Your role will vary in different situations (eg training environment, competition, post-training/competition).

Training environment

In general, most coaching takes place during training, away from the competitive arena. The many hours spent learning new skills, techniques or routines, and developing fitness, strength and conditioning, are vital to the competitive success of your participants.

The exact nature of your role and the amount of time you spend with your participants varies according to their level, age and experience. In the run-up to a competition, your role may change to that of tactician, motivator or adviser.

Competition

Your coaching role also extends into the competitive arena. During competition, you can have a vital influence on the outcome of your participants' performance. You may need to shift roles to observe and analyse performance, and identify tactical or technical errors which your participants may be unaware of. In team sports, you may also have opportunities to make changes

based on your analysis of how things are going (eg substitutions, time-outs, intervals).

Post-training/ competition

After training and competition, you still have an important role to play. You need to analyse your participants' performance to identify what went well and/or not so well, and incorporate this into your planning of future coaching sessions and competitions. If you coach elite performers, you may work alongside advisers and support staff who can assist you (eg sports scientists, performance analysts).

The role of the coach is varied to say the least. On top of your regular coaching duties, you could well find yourself acting as performance analyst, technical adviser, master tactician or assistant official ... not to mention kit bag carrier, caterer and spectator (but hopefully not all at the same time)!

Responsibilities of the coach

As a coach you are in a position of authority and influence, and people will often see you as a role model. It's therefore important that you try to live up to their expectations and that you don't abuse their trust. You should always aim to use your influence positively and ensure that the way in which you coach is safe, responsible and in line with acceptable standards of good practice.

This may all seem a bit daunting at first but, most of the time, it's simply a case of using your common sense. In fact, you're probably aware of most of the safety and ethical issues that exist in sport already.

Your aim as a coach is to stay within the boundaries of good and acceptable practice. Most of your day-to-day coaching activities will probably fall within these boundaries. The key to effective coaching is to actively demonstrate good practice and identify and eliminate poor practice. Understanding more about what constitutes poor practice will help you identify alternative courses of action to ensure that you do this (see Table 1 overleaf).

sports coach UK

Table 1: Examples of good and poor practice

Good practice	Applying recommended standards, being aware of potential risks and taking appropriate action to prevent injury or harm to your participants and yourself	**Examples** • Ensuring that participants warm up thoroughly at the start of each coaching session – this helps to prepare them for training and reduces the risk of injury • Using effective and acceptable methods to help participants develop skills
Poor practice	Can occur as a result of laziness, lack of knowledge or understanding, or simple naivety	**Examples** • Excluding latecomers from the warm-up routine – this could lead to injury during the main part of the session • Using inappropriate methods to develop techniques due to lack of knowledge of other methods

In extreme cases, some aspects of coaching practice may constitute illegal practice – for example:

- Encouraging participants to take illegal performance-enhancing drugs

- Engaging in inappropriate contact or behaviour with young participants.

Promoting good practice

In any profession, whether paid or voluntary, there are accepted and established codes of behaviour and practice to safeguard the welfare of the client and service provider. A code of conduct in coaching is essential to ensure safe, ethical and effective coaching practice.

sports coach UK's *Code of Conduct for Sports Coaches*[1] forms the basis for good coaching practice and is underpinned by the following key principles:

- Rights

- Relationships

- Responsibilities:
  - personal standards
  - professional standards.

It's vital to apply the principles of the code to your coaching. This will ensure that standards are maintained and that coaching is fun and safe for all involved.

7

1 Available from **Coachwise 1st4sport** (tel 0113-201 5555 or visit www.1st4sport.com).

Rights

> Coaches must respect and champion the rights of every individual to participate in sport.

Everyone should have access to sport regardless of gender, age, race, ability, faith or sexual orientation. As a coach you have a duty to ensure that your coaching practice is free from discrimination. It's important to create an environment where everybody has the opportunity to participate to the best of their ability without fear of prejudice or harassment.

Similarly, everyone should have access to coaching. National governing bodies have a duty to ensure that coaching opportunities and qualifications are available to all who wish to pursue them.

Where next?

For further guidance on equity issues in sport, refer to **sports coach UK**'s resource[1] *Equity in Your Coaching.*

Relationships

> Coaches must develop a relationship with athletes (and others) based on openness, honesty, mutual trust and respect.

The relationship between you and your participants is vital to the success of the coaching process. It's important to understand how your participants think and behave – how they learn, how they respond to new instructions and how they deal with winning or losing. This will help you to motivate them and coach new skills. Similarly, in order to respect your instructions, participants need to be familiar with your coaching style, level of knowledge, experience and motives.

The key to developing and maintaining effective working relationships with your participants is good communication and mutual understanding.

---

1   Available from **Coachwise 1st4sport** (tel 0113-201 5555 or visit www.1st4sport.com).

This means being open and honest, and respecting and trusting each other at an appropriate level. It also means being aware of, and taking steps to avoid, the potential danger of developing inappropriate, possibly abusive relationships.

Your aim should be to promote the welfare and best interests of your participants, and to create an environment in which they can contribute to the coaching process and take responsibility for their own decisions.

Children and young people

Children and young people may regard you as a substitute parent and may come to see you first if they have a problem. Your role may change to that of carer, counsellor or listener. It's vital to respond in an ethical manner at all times to prevent your actions being misinterpreted.

Parents

Parents range from the demanding to the protective and, in some cases, the over-protective. Whether demanding or protective,

remember that parents can have a great influence on your young participants.

Parental support is vital for young participants, but good understanding and communication between parents and coaches is essential for this support to be helpful rather than a hindrance. There must be a mutual understanding and acceptance of the roles of parent and coach, and clear lines of demarcation. Parents should not be allowed to take over, dictate or undermine training. On the other hand, you should realise where your responsibility ends and in no way encroach on areas of parental responsibility.

Where next?

For further guidance on establishing effective working relationships with your participants, refer to the following **sports coach UK** resources[1]:

- *Protecting Children: A Guide for Sportspeople*
- *Safe and Sound leaflet.*

1   Available from **Coachwise 1st4sport** (tel 0113-201 5555 or visit www.1st4sport.com).

Responsibilities

Personal standards

> Coaches must demonstrate proper personal behaviour and conduct at all times.

Personal standards relate to the way you behave and conduct yourself when coaching. It's important that you act as a positive role model – this includes things like:

- avoiding the use of abusive language, alcohol and drugs

- maintaining an equal interest in all your participants, even when they are injured or ill

- displaying control, dignity, respect and professionalism at all times

- respecting the rules of your sport(s)

- accepting officials' decisions

- showing good sportsmanship in defeat.

Drug-free sport[1]

The use of performance-enhancing substances or methods (doping) is unfair and contrary to the spirit of fair competition. Drug misuse not only harms participants' health, but severely damages the integrity, image and value of sport, regardless of whether or not the drugs are specifically used to improve performance.

Most participants are in favour of drug-free sport and it's therefore important that they are guided on the use of medication. You can have a significant influence on the decisions they make in this respect. You should constantly reinforce positive values and support your participants through injury or illness by providing acceptable methods of recovery.

- Be consistent in your views about drug-free sport and make it clear to your participants that you expect them to participate fairly and cleanly.

10

1 **sports coach UK** would like to thank UK Sport for its input into this section (see page 35 for contact details).

- Familiarise yourself with the rules that govern the use of substances, particularly when competing in sport at an elite level.
- Encourage participants to appreciate why there are doping rules and why drug-testing is important.

sports coach UK

Professional standards

> To maximise benefits and minimise the risks to athletes, coaches must attain a high level of competence through qualifications and a commitment to ongoing training that ensures safe and correct practice.

As well as maintaining personal standards, you are also responsible for keeping your coaching knowledge up to date. This will help you to continue to provide a safe coaching environment and maintain the respect of your participants and colleagues.

Most national governing bodies provide courses for coaches to update and develop their coaching knowledge, and gain professional recognition for their knowledge and expertise.

11

Where next?

For further guidance on areas of knowledge you need to have as a coach, see pages 25 to 30.

The coaching process

The coaching process should allow participants to achieve their personal goals and may also influence their attitudes, lifestyle, aspirations and abilities. As a coach, you play a major role in planning and leading the three key principles of the process – plan, do and review.

The coaching process is a continuous cycle of:

- observation
- analysis
- goal-setting
- planning
- monitoring
- evaluation
- action planning for the next cycle.

Because the coaching process is continuous, it can start at any point in the cycle. In many cases, several stages will overlap and occur at the same time. All stages are equally important. The coaching process won't be successful if any are missed out or not addressed properly.

ACTION PLANNING

MONITORING AND EVALUATING

OBSERVATION

How will they know they are there?

Where are they now?

PLANNING

ANALYSIS

How are they going to get there?

Where do they want to be?

GOAL-SETTING

Figure 2: Key elements of the coaching process

The key to effective coaching is having a good understanding of the coaching process and being able to apply it.

Relating the questions in the table below to the participants you coach will help you to do this:

Table 2: Applying the coaching process

Question	Suggested action
Where are they now?	• Carry out an initial **observation** of the current level of performance (ie skills and talents that participants already have). • **Analyse** how well the current level of performance matches the ideal model.
Where do they want to be?	• Understand what participants want to achieve. • Establish participants' motivations and commitment to the *journey* ahead. • **Set goals** for participants to work towards.
How are they going to get there?	• **Plan** a series of coaching sessions or an appropriate training programme to enable participants to reach their goals.
How will they know they are there?	• Continually **observe, monitor** and **evaluate** the progress of participants and provide feedback to them. • If goals are achieved, set new, more challenging ones. • If goals are not achieved, identify where things have gone wrong and **re-plan** the programme or **reset** goals.

Planning coaching sessions

> Those who fail to plan,
> plan to fail!

The logical place to start the coaching process is at the planning stage, as the ultimate success of the process relies on effective planning. Key issues to consider when planning your coaching sessions and programmes include:

- coaching environment
- time
- safety
- facilities and equipment.

14

Coaching environment

Create a coaching environment in which your participants can learn, acquire new skills or techniques and improve their performance.

- What are your participants' specific needs and goals for the session?
- What is the ability level of the participants in your group?
- What are your specific goals for the session?
- Do your goals match those of the participants?
- Does the session build on previous sessions?
- Does the session prepare participants for future sessions?
- Does the session include a variety of activities?

sports coach UK

Time

- What time is available?
- Have you allocated sufficient time to each activity to allow participants to achieve the desired level?
- What preparation can you do in advance to ensure the session runs smoothly?

Be constructive with the time available in your session.

Safety

Ensure that the coaching environment is safe.

- What health and safety issues do you need to consider?
- Is first aid provision adequate?

Facilities and equipment

Ensure that you have sufficient and appropriate facilities and equipment.

- What equipment and facilities will you need?
- What safety checks have you carried out?

actionplus

Practical tips

- Provide sufficient time in your sessions for participants to practise and achieve the required level at their pace and learning ability. Don't try to do too much and rush your participants. Select a range of appropriate activities and try to maintain the participants' interest as well as achieve their desired goals.

- Your coaching sessions should be interesting and varied, not boring and repetitive. Participants like to be active and doing different things, rather than just standing around listening to their coach all the time.

- Remember – too much preparation is better than not enough. There's nothing worse than finding yourself halfway through a coaching session and realising that you've already finished everything you planned to do.

Delivering coaching sessions

Once your coaching session is under way, you need to make sure everything's running to plan and that your participants are gaining the maximum benefit. However, effective coaching isn't just about running a series of activities according to a pre-set time plan. Although this is important, you also need to carry out a variety of other tasks at the same time.

These include:

- observing and analysing performance

- planning the next activity

- assessing how well the session is going

- thinking about future developments.

Running a coaching session is a bit of a juggling act, but if you've planned it carefully, this shouldn't be a problem.

Evaluating coaching sessions

> The evaluation of one coaching session marks the start of the planning for the next.

The evaluation stage provides valuable feedback on the performance of both your participants and yourself, which should be carried forwards to the next planning stage.

It's important to invest time in evaluating how sessions have gone and recording your thoughts in some form of logbook for future reference. This will help you to identify activities to repeat and/or avoid in the future, and so strengthen your role as an effective coach. Key issues to consider when evaluating your coaching sessions include:

- participants' progress
- performance against targets
- future targets
- coaching ability.

Participants' progress

Evaluating your coaching sessions will help you to monitor your participant's progress and achievements over a period of time.

- How well did the participants learn the techniques and skills presented to them?
- What developments did each participant demonstrate?

Performance against targets

When evaluating your coaching sessions, compare the actual performance gains with your anticipated targets.

- How well did the session go?
- Did the participants achieve the desired goals?

Future targets

The evaluation stage will help you to set future goals and objectives based on the achievements made by your participants.

- Are the participants ready to progress during the next session?

Coaching ability

The evaluation stage also offers the opportunity to assess your coaching ability and to ensure that your coaching sessions are appropriate and effective.

- What aspects of the session worked well?
- What aspects of the session worked less well?
- How did the participants respond to the instructions given?
- Did the participants show signs of boredom or restlessness?

Where next?

For further guidance on planning, running and evaluating coaching sessions, refer to **sports coach UK**'s resource[1] *How to Coach Sports Effectively.*

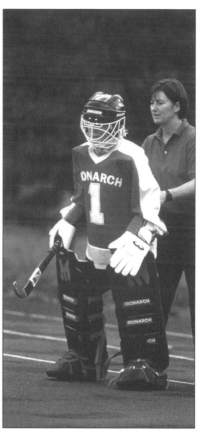

sports coach UK

18

---

1   Available from **Coachwise 1st4sport** (tel 0113-201 5555 or visit www.1st4sport.com).

Why coach?

Knowing why you want to coach will help you to appreciate the different roles and responsibilities described so far in this resource. It will also help you to reflect on your own attitudes, beliefs and motives within your coaching practice.

Who coaches?

All sorts of people from a variety of backgrounds take up coaching for many different reasons. For example, they may be:

- former athletes
- parents/carers of children who participate in a sport
- teachers
- youth leaders
- sports development officers
- people who are interested in sport and keen to help others develop new skills.

Your motives

Why do you want to get into coaching? For yourself or for others, or a combination of the two? Are you more interested in the long-term development of participants or short-term success?

Is your burning ambition to coach a team to cup success or simply to help participants improve their skill levels?

Remember – your participants may not necessarily share the same motives as you. For example, just because you consider a participant to be good enough to join the club team doesn't necessarily mean that she will want to. Her motive for taking part in sport may simply be to get fit or have fun.

Whatever your reason for taking up coaching, you should always adopt a participant-centred approach. This means acting in the interests of your participants, not your own. If your only reason for becoming a coach is personal satisfaction and gain, you're unlikely to be effective and will soon become disappointed and frustrated.

Coaching style

Just as everybody has different reasons for becoming a coach, so everybody adopts a different coaching style depending on their beliefs, values and expectations. Your coaching style will depend on a number of factors but should always reflect good ethical practice.

Coaching style ranges from participant-centred (you adopt a more facilitative role and empower your participants) to coach-centred (directed by you). The style you adopt may vary depending on:

- the group of participants you are working with

- your own personality and coaching philosophy

- the activities

- the environment.

Participant-centred

Adopting a participant-centred approach involves:

- providing leadership

- offering guidance

- sharing decision-making

- guiding participants towards selecting and achieving personal goals.

Coach-centred

Adopting a coach-centred approach involves you making most of the decisions on behalf of your participants and directing activities. This may be appropriate in situations where safety is a critical factor.

Where next?

For further guidance on coaching style refer to the following **sports coach UK** resources[1]:

- *How to Coach Sports Effectively*

- *The Successful Coach: Guidelines for Coaching Practice.*

20

Coaching skills

To be an effective coach and gain the respect and trust of your participants, you need a range of skills including leadership and organisation, communication, teaching and motivation skills.

Leadership and organisation skills

As a coach you need to be:

- well-organised personally
- able to organise and direct other people effectively
- able to organise equipment and facilities safely
- able to demonstrate good leadership skills.

Participants will enjoy safe and well-structured sessions if they know exactly what is expected of them. If you are disorganised, you are more likely to deliver disjointed and unsafe sessions.

Communication skills

Good coaches are always excellent communicators – they may not know everything but can organise and convey their thoughts well. You must be able to communicate effectively with participants, parents, officials and others involved in sport.

You may sometimes feel that, because you possess the relevant knowledge and skills, you must spend all your time giving information and sharing your experiences. However, remember that listening is a vital part of effective communication too.

sports coach UK

Coaches have two ears, two eyes and one mouth, and they should use them in that proportion.

21

As well as giving verbal explanations, you should try to:

* ask questions and listen carefully to the answers

* look closely at what participants do – have they really understood what has been said?

* use demonstrations to convey thoughts or teach new skills (eg teaching a group of novice tennis players how to serve). Make sure that demonstrations are correct – otherwise performers will learn poor techniques and pick up bad habits

* be aware of the non-verbal messages you send – gestures, facial expressions and body language can convey even more powerful messages than the spoken word. If a participant has performed a task well, a smile will help enforce the learning of a new skill. During competition, verbal communication is not always permitted and the use of body language can help participants cope with difficult situations.

> Remember that actions speak louder than words – ensure your body language and behaviour match your words.

Teaching skills

Improving an individual's performance in sport involves some teaching. You need to help people understand new information and learn new skills. To do this, you need to select different teaching methods to suit the:

* type of learner (eg beginner or expert)

* activity (eg introducing a new technique, teaching a team tactic or improving physical preparation).

Good coaches get the best from their participants by making appropriate choices about what, how and when to teach a particular skill or technique. It's important to progress in short, simple, logical steps from one part of the session to the next and at a pace that suits most of the participants.

A disorganised session will soon create restlessness and irritation either through boredom or frustration. You must make learning both exciting and rewarding.

Motivational skills

You should not have to motivate participants as they will usually motivate themselves. What you must do is create and manage a coaching environment that encourages self-motivation. Use your communication skills to find out what motivates your participants to take part in sport and drives them to improve performance. Self-motivating factors might be to:

- have fun

- meet people

- compete

- keep fit and healthy

- meet a challenge

- please others (eg parents and friends)

- gain a reward (eg a title, a trophy, money)

- have a good self-image

- achieve dreams.

Do you know why participants take part in your sport?

Participants are more likely to gain enjoyment and remain involved in sport if it fulfils their needs. Get to know your participants and their needs – these may change due to various factors (eg leaving school and starting work). Remember, your participants' needs should be of primary concern.

To stimulate the motivation and development of your participants, you must select the right approach. At times you will have to praise, cajole, discipline, criticise and challenge your participants – this may not always be an easy task.

23

Administration skills

Inevitably, you may dislike the amount of time taken up with the administration of your coaching programmes. Try to find other people (eg parents of participants, sports club committee members) who could help to take care of various administrative tasks, ranging from booking facilities to arranging transport.

Whoever takes responsibility should remember that sound planning and good organisation are essential to the smooth and effective running of your coaching programme. In carrying out your administrative functions, you should demonstrate standards and behaviour that set positive examples to the people you coach. Never leave things to the last minute and never take things for granted.

Additional skills

You may already be thinking of other roles that you are called upon to play and the various skills you will need to fulfil them. You may need to be a friend, social worker, publicity agent, negotiator, scientist or student. Whatever role you play, recognise its importance and the responsibilities it carries. If you need assistance in fulfilling a role or developing new skills, seek it. Be curious and search for solutions.

> Acknowledging your limitations is a strength, not a weakness.

sports coach UK

Coaching knowledge

To be an effective coach, able to plan, deliver and evaluate coaching sessions and programmes, you need to supplement the skills described in the previous section with up-to-date knowledge in many areas.

There is no substitute for having a sound knowledge of your sport, the participants you coach, the factors that influence performance and the factors that influence the way you coach (see Figure 3).

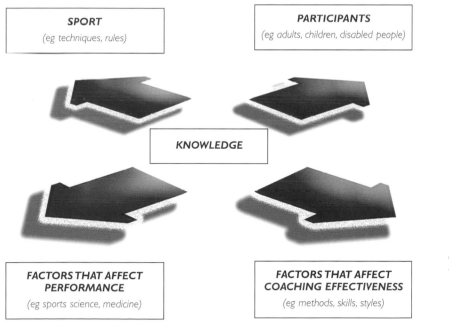

Figure 3: Areas of coaching knowledge

The areas of knowledge you need include:

- **technical and tactical** – a full understanding of the techniques, skills and coaching methods that work best in your sport

- **psychological and sociological** – knowing how people learn, think and interact in their sport

- **communication** – the ability to explain, listen, demonstrate and present information

- **monitoring** – observing, recording, organising and summarising information

- **fitness and training** – an understanding of how the body responds to exercise and training

- **health** – an understanding of how to promote and support a healthy lifestyle

- **safety and first aid** – the ability to adopt safe practices and prevent injury

- **participants** – the ability to guide and motivate them to enjoy participation and competition, control anxiety, cope with success and failure, achieve personal goals and fulfil their potential[1].

You shouldn't expect to be an expert in every area. However, gaining some knowledge of each area will help you develop the many skills involved in coaching. In seeking out new knowledge, skills and understanding, you will become better at monitoring and evaluating your own performance – an important step towards becoming a better coach.

actionplus

---

1   It is particularly important when coaching children to have a thorough knowledge of child growth and development, as well as how to protect children.

Techniques, skills and tactics

As a coach, you need a comprehensive knowledge of the techniques, skills and tactics of your sport. **Technique** means how to execute a particular action. A **skill** is the application of technique(s) within specific situations.

Techniques need to be introduced and coached in the correct sequence. You must be able to pass on information about techniques, skills and tactics at an appropriate level for those with whom you are working. You should also know how and when to use different techniques, and how to help your participants choose the correct tactics and skills for a variety of situations.

At first you should limit the range of different techniques, skills and tactics you introduce – otherwise participants will struggle to make the right choice at the required time.

As participants' abilities and experiences improve, the range of options can be gradually increased. You must be able to analyse techniques, skills and tactics, and be able to help your participants develop them. By performing this role effectively, your participants will become self-reliant and independent.

sports coach UK

27

Current fitness and training practices

Success in any sport involves being prepared and trained for a specific event or activity. One important role of the coach is to help participants achieve the levels of physical and mental fitness required for successful involvement in their chosen sport. Fitness is a participant's ability to cope mentally (mind) and physically (body) with the demands placed upon them. It's developed through appropriate training sessions that make increasing demands on the participant and so forces the body or mind to adapt to that level of demand.

To be a good coach, you need to know:

- how the body works

- the effects of training on the efficiency of the body

- how the mind works

- how mental skills can be improved

- how to construct training sessions that will develop these elements.

For further guidance, refer to the following **sports coach UK** resources[1]:

- *The Body in Action*

- *How to Coach Sports Effectively*.

actionplus

---

1   Available from **Coachwise 1st4sport** (tel 0113-201 5555 or visit www.1st4sport.com).

Staying up to date

Knowledge and skills must be kept up to date. You can do this in a variety of ways:

- Personal practice and experience

- Regular contact and discussion with other coaches and experts about important issues that affect sport (eg drugs, overtraining, current trends and practices, ethics, officials and rules)

- Working with a mentor (eg a qualified and experienced coach)

- Reading coaching resources (eg **sports coach UK**[1], national governing bodies)

- Reviewing material from abroad or from related sports

- Attending coach education courses (eg **sports coach UK**, national governing bodies)

- Becoming a member of coaching organisations (eg **sports coach UK**[2]).

sports coach UK

29

---

1 Available from **Coachwise 1st4sport** (tel 0113-201 5555 or visit www.1st4sport.com).

2 Contact **sports coach UK** Membership Services for further details (tel 0113-290 7612).

Keeping your knowledge up to date will help you to continue to provide a safe coaching environment and maintain the respect of your participants and colleagues.

Don't be afraid to look to others for advice and guidance, both inside and outside sport. And don't be afraid to admit what you don't know. Take advantage of every opportunity to learn new skills and update your knowledge. Most importantly, you should take pleasure from your coaching activities, whether you are a professional or a volunteer.

If you have an enquiring and open mind, you can develop innovative techniques, tactics and attitudes, which will affect the way your sport is practised and coached in the future. Effective coaches maintain their curiosity and quest for knowledge. They challenge traditional wisdom and beliefs in the search for improvement and understanding, and welcome change with a critical eye.

> You only become effective when you can successfully apply your knowledge.

actionplus

Where next?

Coaching is first and foremost about people. Encouraging them to enjoy the positive benefits of sport and helping them to achieve their potential is very challenging for coaches.

To be an effective coach, you will need to fulfil a number of different roles and accept a variety of responsibilities. You will also need a good understanding of the coaching process and how to apply it, so that you adopt a participant-centred approach at all times. In addition, you will need to possess a wide range of skills and up-to-date knowledge in many areas. This will help to ensure that your coaching is safe, responsible and in line with acceptable standards of good practice.

This may seem daunting and you certainly shouldn't expect to become an expert overnight. However, if you fulfil the criteria above (or have the potential to do so), you have the raw materials required to become an effective coach. With appropriate guidance and relevant experience, you can have a positive influence on the development of your participants, both as performers and as people.

sports coach UK (scUK) offers a variety of workshops and resources related to coaching.

Workshops

- How to Coach Sports Effectively
- How to Coach Sports Safely
- Coaching Methods and Communication
- Equity in Your Coaching
- Goal-setting and Planning
- Good Practice and Child Protection

For more information about these workshops, contact your nearest Regional Training Unit (RTU). RTU contact details are available from **scUK** (tel 0113-274 4802 or visit www.sportscoachuk.org).

Resources

The following resources are available from **Coachwise 1st4sport** (tel 0113-201 5555 or visit www.1st4sport.com):

- Crouch, M and Lester, G et al (2002) **Protecting children: a guide for sportspeople**. 3rd edition. Leeds, Coachwise Solutions. ISBN 0 947850 50 3

- Hazeldine, R (1987) **The body in action.** 2nd edition. Leeds, National Coaching Foundation. ISBN 0 947850 51 1

- Kerr, A (2001) **Equity in your coaching**. Leeds, Coachwise Solutions. ISBN 1 902523 41 5

- National Coaching Foundation (1996) **Coaching sessions: a guide to planning and goal-setting**. Leeds, National Coaching Foundation. ISBN 0 947850 35 X

- National Coaching Foundation (1996) **The successful coach: guidelines for coaching practice**. Leeds, National Coaching Foundation. ISBN 0 947850 16 3

- **sports coach UK** (2001) **Code of conduct for sports coaches**. Leeds, Coachwise Solutions.

- **sports coach UK** (updated 2001) **Safe and sound** (leaflet). Leeds, Coachwise Solutions.

Other resources in the *Coaching Essentials* series[1] include:

How to Coach Sports Safely

Focusing on safe practice in sport, this resource clearly outlines the health and safety issues associated with coaching. Includes new sections on managing risk and manual handling. Essential guidance for every coach. (Based on *Safety and Injury.*)

How to Coach Sports Effectively

This resource includes practical tips to help develop coaching skills and allow participants to get the most benefits from your sessions. Also features chapters on planning, organising and delivering sessions. Everything you need to be an effective coach. (Based on *Planning and Practice.*)

How to Coach Children in Sport

Aimed at anyone working with children in sport, this easy-to-read resource presents the basic principles of good practice and introduces the concept of long-term athlete development. (Based on *Working With Children.*)

How to Coach Disabled People in Sport

This resource tackles all the frequently asked questions posed by sports teachers, coaches and participants about how to work with disabled sportspeople. As well as a whole spectrum of new ideas for inclusion, the resource will introduce and offer guidance to any coach involved with disabled people in sport. (Based on *Working With Disabled Sportspeople.*)

where next?

33

---

1 Available from **Coachwise 1st4sport** (tel 0113-201 5555 or visit www.1st4sport.com).

Useful contacts

sports coach UK

sports coach (scUK) works closely with national governing bodies to provide a comprehensive service for coaches throughout the UK. This includes an extensive programme of workshops which have proved valuable to coaches from all types of sport and every level of experience. For details of **scUK** workshops in your area, contact your nearest Regional Training Unit. For more information about **scUK**'s workshops and other services, contact:

sports coach UK
114 Cardigan Road
Headingley
Leeds LS6 3BJ
Tel: 0113-274 4802
Fax: 0113-275 5019

E-mail
coaching@sportscoachuk.org
Website
www.sportscoachuk.org

National governing bodies

The national governing body for your sport or activity will give advice on coaching courses and other relevant information. National governing body contact details are available from:

Central Council of Physical Recreation (CCPR)
Francis House
Francis Street
London
SW1P 1DE
Tel: 020-7854 8500
Fax: 020-7854 8501

E-mail:
info@ccpr.org.uk
Website
www.ccpr.org.uk

UK Sport

UK Sport's Drug Information Database provides comprehensive guidance on the status of medications and substances licensed in the UK. UK Sport has also produced a wide range of drug-free sport resources. Subjects covered include:

- testing procedures
- prohibited substances
- why some athletes may misuse drugs
- national anti-doping policy.

UK Sport Drug Information Line
Tel: 0800-528 0004
(free phone)

UK Sport Drug Information E-mail
drug-free@uksport.gov.uk

UK Sport Drug Information Database
www.uksport.gov.uk/did

35

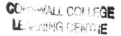